The Land of Green Ginger

ANTONY ROWLAND was born in Bradford in 1970. Since studying at Hull and Leeds he has taught literature and creative writing at The University of Salford. He has published poems in various journals and magazines, including *Critical Quarterly*, *Stand* and *P.N. Review*. A selection of his work appeared in *New Poetries III* (Carcanet, 2002). He received an Eric Gregory Award in 2000, and a Learning Northwest Award in 2001.

The Land of Green Ginger

Antony Rowland

SALT

CAMBRIDGE

PUBLISHED BY SALT PUBLISHING
PO Box 937, Great Wilbraham, Cambridge CB21 5JX United Kingdom

All rights reserved

© Antony Rowland, 2008

The right of Antony Rowland to be identified as the
author of this work has been asserted by him in accordance
with Section 77 of the Copyright, Designs and Patents Act 1988.

This book is in copyright. Subject to statutory exception
and to provisions of relevant collective licensing agreements,
no reproduction of any part may take place without the written
permission of Salt Publishing.

First published 2008

Printed and bound in the United Kingdom by Biddles Ltd, King's Lynn, Norfolk

Typeset in Swift 9.5 / 13

*This book is sold subject to the conditions that it shall not,
by way of trade or otherwise, be lent, re-sold, hired out,
or otherwise circulated without the publisher's prior consent
in any form of binding or cover other than that in which
it is published and without a similar condition including this
condition being imposed on the subsequent purchaser.*

ISBN 978 1 84471 400 1 hardback

Salt Publishing Ltd gratefully acknowledges
the financial assistance of Arts Council England

1 3 5 7 9 8 6 4 2

for Alan and Emma

Contents

Engrish	1
Pie	2
A History of the Beard	4
The Italian Bob	6
Engrish	8
Kwak	11
Lekke-Bekke	13
Damrak	14
Croky	16
Vienna	17
Scallops	18
The Cake	21
Charlie and Sassoon	23
The Long Cyclops	25
Cucumber	26
Cwm	28
Ox	29
Rain-pie	30
The Flies' Cemetery	32
1926	34
Ganton Mount	35
Mistle from 1900	36
Pomfret	37
Cromwell's Toothbrush	38
Primigravida	40
Polly	42
The Land of Green Ginger	43
Cech Speaks	44
Golem	45

Terezín	46
Rowland on the Hair	47
Lésvos	49
Skála Eressou	50
Bogue	51
Io	53
Gently Michael	55
Chestnut Avenue	56
Tongue and Udder	57
Moose	59
Press-ganged	60
R.A.F. Mapless	61
I.M. Deltics, 1977–81	62
London Particular	63
Suffrage	65

Acknowledgements

Some of the poems first appeared in the following magazines and anthologies: *Citizen 32*, *Critical Quarterly*, *Leviathan Quarterly*, *New Poetries III* (Carcanet, 2002), *PN Review*, *Poetry Salzburg Review*, *Psychopoetica*, *Stand*, *Staple* and *Yorkshire Journal*. I would like to thank the staff at Chetham's Library and the John Ryland's Library (Deansgate) in Manchester, Sue Powell for her books, and Scott Thurston, for all those ginger adventures.

Engrish

Beard papa pursues handmade deliciousness
The deliciousness of handmade cooking
Is not in proportion to the good point of the tool
It is in proportion to affection of the person who cooks
Happiness if help of the handmade cooking which
Affection was put into can be done at all, marinate retard.
The small pigs which carry happiness convey a feeling to everybody.
Give your friends your wonderful feeling recollections
That it travelled this ground with this chocolate.
I shall enjoy your space combining various items
Since it seems that the sun is wrong. After all, dream is a fair wind.
There are some nice goods nearby: beam happily; pray for a miracle.
A selection of gentlemen: from now on I want no more time competition.
Please purchase goods after affirmation: shopping is always taking care of
    me;
I shall recompense it before long. So many alligators, so many dreams:
All are grittering, aren't they? You lady will push this button before leaving.
Let's go out in a poetry mood, since I like you in the recent days.
Do you like bowling? Breaking down the pins and get hot communication?
I am absorbed in a naughty act of nature, jyu-jyu:
Let's enjoy smoking and keep manner, produce a young party exceedingly
(we support your socks).
I depart with my full bag of time
I wish to sing a duet with transparent time
I'm glad to know you're fine
This is about all I want to tell you this time
Time seems to return to the turn of its beautiful melody
Please listen to the dream flow a fresh heart discloses
Please look at my fresh face
Please receive it just when you open your heart
A bouquet to all of you all over the world.
Listen, do you believe when I say?

Pie

'Will you go to the pie-feast?'
— Dodsley, 1550

Singing herb singe roast vapours Fray: Saturday
pie-floater in Rawson market; waxy peas island
gelatine-coated pink flush before comic stall.
Passionate friendship wanted with a Bentos,
good sense of meat to gravy ratio. Slim,
attractive suet looking for pudding love
with like-minded crust: no tin wasters;
Swiss-slapped pâté on the brawn of pigley
-pie, ridged with needle precision and oh,
so delicately browned at the knobs, bow-tie
at the centre hot-puddled, pie *de pundio*,
fayre buttys of Porke smyte with Vele welcome.
Mint-chopped sausage baguette found abandoned:
police are savouring bent *expenditum*
at Bolton Priory in pyis et pastellis. Pie-purrs
undercut by cholesterol scam: police support nut diet.
Sought in attractive wastes of Uppermill: chips just so,
clay-coloured dish Delia-thick in hot top-slick
— 'That's not a pie, it's boo-gloop with a bin lid' —
pastry chocked round oval but peels off faced with fork.
'Hote pies, hote! Goode gees and grys, Gowe dyne, Gowe!'
Bramble for afters? No, two would be spoiling us.
Policy wonks hit pies with fat tax, fatties
who puttis fast at their vly pyiss, headlines
Yorkshire chippies' favourite rag, *The Fryer*.
Finger buffet threat to national health:
Blair's babes weaned on focaccia and lamb's lettuce
forced into Mowbray tour of the bow-walled pie,
northern one-portion growlers and stand-pies
that stand-pipe Robert's pie-house in Bradford:
Jerry bombs cobweb the glass but daily displays
defiantly steam. 'Every puff', puffed Priestley,

'was defying Hitler. Keep your pie level
to avoid ungelled gravy dribble incident.'
The Fryer pastes the government's attempt
to ration meat dripping—'Animal fat
for the dominant race. Animal fat
for the dominant county within that race.'
Cold balls lovingly brisked with milk yolk: Sunday chow
brought family together not gristle niblets
in bad butchers' pork cast-offs. Bison pies
go missing in Salford posse mix up. Small shops'
warmers in sausage roll chaffage scandal:
police inspect gluten levels, mustard lovers,
cuckoo mayonnaise run off with sheer pie.

A History of the Beard

'The master of the barber shop practised surgery and could breathe
a vein as well as mow a beard'
— *Antiquarian Repertory*

That's blood in my window, yes. Forget it. Let me cover you with the
    suds of a laver,
curleth you with a Crisping Iron and (on the side) cutteth you with a
    Knife
so that the Blood spitteth. You say you only came in for a mullet,
not phlebotomy? Sit still. Prepare to be frounst with my irons
while you strum on the gittern. I see your ambrosial locks are an old
    cast.
Do not worry. With this camphor soap I shall tweak your inamorato's
    peak
and trim it as tight as your subercles. (That's sidies.) Your mowchatows
will wither their tendrils: I shall trim you like a cheese.
Would you like a gentleman's cut? I see not.
A common cut? County cut? Court cut? Shall I fix a wig with the doup
    of a candle,
cannikin and dredging box? A periwig on the pow, weel-heeled, sansy
and as decent as that of my friend Sir Thomas Browne, so large it
    loaded a camel?
A bag-wig with sausage curls? A campaign-wig with knobs, bobs or
    dildos?
Are you are a Puritan? Do you want a commode on your head? If so,
there shall be no tricking, trimming, rubbing, scratching, combing,
    clawing, trickling,
toying to tawe out tuppence. Instead, I shall boss your mouth with the
    lather
of my balls (sweet sope balls) and ferret your molars as in Gay's fable,
'The Goat Without a Beard', in which 'Black, rotten teeth' are strung
to dry in the window by the cups of blood. No? God save you, then,
from the women barbers of Scarborough. As my friend St Jerome said,
'The woman who wears a wig commits a moral sin', as if
it were the barnet of Pepys, made with the hair of the plague.

[4]

Go and comb your peruke in an opera box, beaux-face.
Make haste and shave on a Sunday, be fined like that naughty Patrick
Brontë in Thornton. On the Lord's Day, indeed, sir, espied by Dissenters.
No, sir, I shall hear nothing against Sir Thomas More,
who cast his beard aside from the chopping block with his last words:
'It hath done no treason'. So the ballad goes: 'It is very hard to handle a
    beard'
whether dagger-like or stiletto, that might eyes outpike.
I can see this is all irrelevant natter. Sir, you have a chin like a nutmeg.
You would fair well in the Hum-hums of Afghanistan, where the
    humble being
yanks at the sovereign's bush, to heap complaints on the shame of the
    beard.
No, I do not keep spares. Never demand a beard of another,
pull the devil by the beard, make anyone's beard, beard someone,
or wipe the beard of the sister of King Henry the Eighth. Starch it
    instead. Ah, I see: you
have no head. Well, God speed you, my love, and remember this advice:
to protect the beard from disarrangement, always wear a cardboard box
    at night.

The Italian Bob

'Poorer people would go to a travelling barber, who set down a
stool beneath a tree.'
— JANE ASSER

The wimples of my mind begin. The syntax of the haircut
must unfold as you spill me your desires and I give you leaves
in a teacup. I could perm you like the stories of the crispines
of the rich, the polled bobs, swallow-tail beards and pompadour pads,
or cork to plump old cheeks; lappets of mouse skin skinned for
    eyebrows.
For you, a basin under chestnuts that swell like heads, the negatives
of leaves imprinted on your seat. You sniff at my pestilence,
tales of square beards worn by Egyptian queens at court,
but if barbers have sunk as low as this bower today, then why
did the Egyptian gods hire a barber god? You drone about your job
when I have clipped among the frescoes of seaweed, then baited bulls
in ancient Crete, heavy with unguents. Us sibyls bached
and diademed ourselves with carats chignon crinoline-kisses ear-scoops
until my lovers faded into the Sumerian curls in the graves at Ur:
I cried over the mussel shells of eye shadow and rouge.
Would you *wish* to know that Stuart women rarely wear a hat? But oh,
    those melon
heads of the Restoration, small cauls restored by the bun at the back.
Your snores make me feel like a firework on the sixth:
you won't get that, and I am aghast by my foreknowledge
of your bouffant to be. I shall slake your knots with pomatum,
tonsure or flocculate until you wake. No, I am not the daughter of Samos,
Claros, Delos or Delphi. And leave my sheep alone.
This stool is the stone I used to mount when the portents flowed
time after time. My words stitch it, like the nine prophecies
for Tarquinius Superbus. Apollo gave me years,
the same number of grains I could salve in my palms, but forgot
to ask for youth; he bartered for my cherry in exchange.
Each week I wizen. My breasts crumple to a cicada.
When my knuckles crumble in these scissor-holes

I shall be hung in a cage at Cumae, a bore on the history
and future of the follicle. The gods will jibe, 'Sibyl, what do you want?'
I throw them a broken teacup then squeak, 'I want to die.'

Engrish

I will eat this and will become fortunate all together
the thing eat delicious is happy
therefore it will make a living happily
its colour and texture make a room of peace.
We, tasty place, choose very carefully to bring you
what you haven't appreciated ever, braised dork.
This is the most comfortable meal you have ever run into,
beard papa freshness and deliciousness:
everybody, even a family, will be continued every day;
future voices need to be heard — eyebrows are always.
Don't take out a hand! You could sleep very comfortably.
We cheer everybody who communicates with all the heart,
that's why our products are always alive. This
portable food becomes automatically portable when carried.
Ah, hamburger friend: I feel happiness when I eat him.

Put on one's thinking cap — being delicious is not everything.
Because now only happens once,
wear the scent of freshly pickled roses:
refreshing fragrance sends you a comfortable time,
wraps you in excellent function and the refined touch quality.
Anticipation of a wonderful encounter! Hopes are at my side,
my dream that has begun to move.
I smell the smelly smell of something that smells smell:
happiness since you were in me — I am the fortunate!
But a man's oath are wafers: he ploughs in sand and sows
against the wind who hopes for constant. Changeable.
Man is changeable. Weathercock. Men wind and fire
are ever changing. Slack and bitter, the game of life.
You found a treasure at last — I have only a faint memory
of that affair. The scene still comes to mind
now and then. I have a vividly remember seeing you here.
Let's walk to the next town in the night:

warmth of a tree is told as it is, to favourite you of wooden goods.
Love — no surfing! Here is dangerous area — sharks get charmed you.
Why shouldn't we kill the people?

Still — hello, my friend. Friendship makes a happiness double:
let's divide sadness half and make us remove our unhappiness fears.
We think it will always be with smile. Then, a pleasant thing comes.
There is something going on deep in the forest,
so get ready for infinity, enchanted freak.
We'll advise you about your stickiness about your daily life:
our brand makes a thing which a consumer is satisfied.
All around us, our own world of wonder! Can't you see how chic we are?
For the sake of irreplacable persons, we'll dramatise an extravagance:
under the sea all fishes are romantic vagabonds, travel the fantastic
    world.

Two new conditions to live — harmony and mildness. My shop is your
    friend,
but carrying out to other floors and carrying in should be withheld.
The life in the world of value is done, the point of view of the thing
which was different from the general person and the way of thinking.
Humanity are fighting against tired:
avoid seniority dribble, make a garden an insignificant stage,
a dream catcher. Beware, I'm armed and have tension.
And particular about the material
And particular about the material
and addition things such as an antiseptic never used for health
which creates a healing time and space beyond reality for you.
Very few people cannot know this by now;
however, we are informing you again to be sure.
The reason why is that products can be very active in a variety of scene
such as a site of construction, party and something like that.
Please, no conversation, no saliva

Please pull a string when you swell manually
Pleasure is born here, unintentionally with individuality,
nonchalantly with sensibility. Take a pause; have a rest—then
look back yourself and reconsider. My flowers in recollection
sing a poem in sepia color. Swarms of winter gnats
are still around here, gently warbling and chittering.
Pleasant things . . . I really love them! I'm in a very fine mood.
All are new. Glory be to God for dappled things,
for skies of couple-color and a brinded cow.
You are available at the ticket office. Thank you.

Kwak

I am supping from a Bunsen burner,
your eyes that go on forever,
the frisson of always being about to eat.
Ushered into a Winstub, where the munster
will not be served until the cheese walks
on the tarte flambée, the minster
melts in your background, the kwak
beer yeasts, you supper me.

I stand at the painting you were two days ago:
these chocolate hearts laced in tiroirs are
the thoughts of small lovers. An orphan
made your face then snaffled your confiture
with the mint finger of the statue
parked in the Barrage Vauban,
about to rouge her lips, too engorged
and separated from the clutch.

I could have strangled that giraffe
as you gave me the gist of your eyes,
Frisk mints, and my stomach bloomed,
knotted at your recognition of a scene.
Please do not stand next to anybody
in a gallery. I cannot stand it.
'Monsieur, vous cherchez une idée?'
'Voulez-vous une giraffe?'

We breakfast on the thumb, Au Coin du Feu,
as I regard you en coin, from a corner,
the corner of your eyes, you have cornered
my heart, 'Have I seen you in a corner?',
l'épicerie du coin, the local grocer,
certainly, yes, dans the coin, but you will never
be round about, I'm not pas du coin,
from here, nor are ... if only I could jam you.

Fifteen minutes with you, the bones
of your cheeks conker my thoughts
as the snail shells bicker around us.
I am crocked, monsieur. You lean in:
'Are you permanent?'; 'Would you enjoy
a bloc of goose?' You rule. The raindrops
are coming down like stair-rods. Mint.
The gargoyles are streaming. Look at you.

Lekke-Bekke

We reflect on pouting windows
in the slippery dawn: ice wrinkles
the seamy pavements. Flesh for hire
on the Velvet Canal: enticing taps
near cold Vondel's house, Aesthetic Nails
and Computer Winkel. Sending mints
was an act of betrayal. We're hours
from your lips in the Nijmegen winter.

There, the kwak girl's lekke-bekke
beaks steaming creamy frothy coffee:
we kiss by the frozen fish gobs,
and the kussen-sloop of sloping desire.
'Have you any odd-sized packages?'
Yesterday's shoes one foot from yours,
sated by the tong stall and market pinks.
The coley soils our fingers like wet coal.

Welcome to the sleep seats, Schiphol airport,
facing budget planes, our absent future.
Precarious pears of unknown nationality
ripple the carts' tiers, my rapid eyes.
Minding the gap between my bags
and your city, you declare a marriage.
Polders lower like mood, estimation
of security throwing my pack, a bouquet.

Damrak

White rabbits greet the eve of September
on Rokin, a street which leaves a hole
in Amsterdam. Our temporary home
is shabby as the fubs in The Flying Dutchman;
our carpets are the texture of droog brood.
In our rucksack, a nibble of cracker packets.
Autumn comes with a creeping hush.

This city is a giddy kipper.
This bridge is lekker in an icing of stream.
Crepuscular roads of water are
dreamed by seekers of skunk;
fingers twitch in bottomless pockets.
Dante's waterways concentricised Hell;
the lidless eyes of tourists pass.

Your face as grey as an absent tulip,
we grace Damrak, stationed by a rusp of canals.
A heron freezes the obelisk of a barge.
Pigeons boozle loose air in Singel.
ECUs rise like metaphysical bees
from these thin roofs atop with hooks.
The single sun is a Gogh, ocherous.

The waiters are as elusive as ciscos
in the brown bar, The Three Quarks, marking
the discos of Dam Square. Round the Vondelpark:
flesh, sand and guitars, all bad.
The fat porks glisten in the Indian heat.
In the Twin Pigs, banana bunches peek
like yellow spiders over the bowls.

We have forgotten your mother for a night
but the hotel is still the edge of a nightmare.
Our nostrils pickle with Damrak's sough

as, reflecting neon, mushrooms and windows,
our owner gnomes on Warmoesstraat
with Sunday smiles and hosepipes.
An aubade of dealers flushes the cobbles.

Croky

'Jim Morrison is not here'
— Sign, Montparnasse Cemetery

It seemed obscene to snack on Croky in the cemetery
of Père Lachaise, oh holy father of the chair
who did not say, In the midst of death
we are not in life, so I dream of lobsters,
les homards on skates of ice, Chez Clovis.
As quick as an eye, you winced
when seated by a tank of sellotaped claws.

They were taking forty winks. Gérard de Nerval
pamped his lobster 'on a lead down rue des Beaux Arts'
but did poodles bark at the crustacean and his barking homme?
Our peur at their unblinking, fishy eyes was not
the metaphysics of a dunderbumble or Cluny, it was
the idealism of dolls, like that dream
you weaned your mother off her immanent crash.

Montparnasse is not a Jimless 'bone and stone dump'
but fruits de mer that bob in the heat-shimmer.
My dinner is no longer a dream.
I did not want to end like this but
there are homard et huîtres in my freezer.
In the midst of its detox, I reach for a knife.
Can a lobster ken its future bisque?

Vienna

'The average Austrian is happy with some soup followed by
Palatschinken (sweet pancakes), *Topfenstrudel* (special cheesecake) or
Apfelstrudel; a huge variety of sweet or savoury *Knödel* (dumplings);
pasta with eggs or sweet pasta with nuts or poppy seeds. However,
tourists are offered *Schnitzel* . . .'
— Fatima Martin, Surrey

A shrine for Eagles. Fascism.
Coffee with frothy bite and shots
and cake where no one dares eat it
save the unforeigned, unafraid of fat,
the blood of Blutwurst, the sour of Kraut,
and Hitler's glaze down Schottenring, a lance
clocked in the Schatzkammer that launched his creed.

Clouds glipped with sun pass the Oper, red.
No one reads print squinted in Resistance museums,
paragons to Communist virtue, Austria a victim,
whereas the Kunsthaus gluts with camera flash
and lamps too expensive to own. Alone,
Hundertwasser's paint splashes clash with clear Dunkelbier
and soot that felts the fuzz of St Stephen's roof.

Vienna is a cathedral
stained with windows of indelible history,
Babel above, as tourists sift the isles sacked
by the fossilised offal of catacombs below.
Waiting in Albertinaplatz, hosted by cherubs,
an iron Jew rests by empty monuments.
He is still, scrubbing.

Scallops
i.m. Charles Rowland, 1896–1982

'In their children do the Parents liue (in a manner) after their
death ... leave collops of their owne flesh aliue behind them.'
—J. ROGERS, *Gl. Godly Loue*

'Scollop potatoes in a Dutch oven, with bread and cream, butter
and condiments.'
—MRS RAFFALD, *English House-Keeper*

The perversion in our family
of Mrs Raffald's scallops. 'Scallops'—
testaceous animals: cousins of
the holy cockle, blushing Prawne, Wilke
and well-armed Oyster; the pilgrim's cockle worn
like a pebble-cairn from the shrine of St James
of Compostella, garnyschyd wt scalepps.
'Collop Monday'—the day before Shrove Tuesday
when only eggs and bacon are tossed
into a huge sandwich. The collop-cake.

You had never tasted the peat
of Laphroaig before a hoary officer
pressed a whisky into your lap:
Wesleyan, teetotal, you never looked
back. Now your men are chippy, pining for
the hoydens and chippies on Woodhouse Moor.
You long for your mother's scallops,
potatoes chipped across then fried,
bitten under slices of virgin bread
with vinegar. 'I'll cut you into collops!'

You can put it on paper, will volunteer
for tanks and sea pie in the heaven of Wool
and Lulworth cove after Ypres. Meanwhile,
you pad the mud to the dressing station,
shoulder to shoulder in the stubble ground.

The sunset kindles where once was a wood.
Highlanders keek from cattle trucks,
tartan limbs preserved by chlorine gas.
Rats swim in dugs of mud, taste
your bayonets and die with babies' shrieks.

The Geordies sing for their singing hinnies.
A young collop who called for wine last night
in an unroofed church and sang 'Until'
till all decongregated into the silent night
is sucked into a bog of scallop-
toed coots. A blunder is a rifle
the wrong way round: the helping hand
goes off below the belt. Now rats
are silent and the sycamores orange
around the hoar-frosts of the Somme.

Chocolate comes up before each push
and stars that guide the new CO
from Savile Row, but with his fingers
on the nebulae. But oh, those Prussians,
the grabbing party with 'potato mashers'
that always leave someone clutching
their foot. Whale oil arrives for frostbite
but all your boots are logged in the floor:
you curse them with a missing asterisk.
'In Demi-Lune, watered to the waist!'

An abandoned kirk deconsecrates
as you snore through the whizz-bangs to Arras,
then zigzag past the listening post.
You tug at your heels to speak
in No Man's Land, rag a chap
from Lancashire, sniped through the buttocks.
His hands are a half-sheet of paper,

gift-wrapping the collop of a martyr.
You relieve the Yorkshire hussars who say
'See you at 'top of those Briggate stairs!'

The stairs were a convenience.
Hodge. Zonnebeke. Boezinge. Menin Road.
'Get your shovels; parkin's coming up!',
rock buns from Bradford with a note:
'These rocks are b***y hard. Sharpen your teeth.'
You joke about your number, the gold
letters of your name above the stave,
how it might come on this scalloped plain
as the timbre of the guns shivers
the timber of your friends that cross the knoll.

What bad use was your engine for?
The collops of cavalry horses
swell in the mud. The crew goes west
of another 'bus' on Vimy Ridge;
your hope dwindles to a ghost as
you laugh like skulls in the estaminet.
Then, one hundred and five days before
the collop-cake, the miracle of an egg
for armistice breakfast, your grins
as wide as teeth on your beaten faces.

The Cake
i.m. Jack Marsland

'Mi feet's cauld, mi shoon's thin, gie's mi cakes and let's rin'
— Hogmanay rhyme, 1864

Baffled by the mellow cream,
all day with the smell of apples
in your head instead of a bullet
and Blunden's homely cattle-cake,
you sight your boots towards the trench,
your soles to trace the shell-holes home.

A cake for a life: the gift
of a cake in the trenches.
Under the moon-slice, hours
until dawn, the package from Leeds,
that gnawed your dreams of warmer feet,
forgiving shoes among the rats.

Jack cursed all serges as cakes,
their bespoke battles all to cock:
too green round the flappers for him
('no artillery—just bayonets?!')
Charles knew their cake'd 'av it's dough';
Jack bagged his cake with his ammo.

The trench was caked with dawn
at Zero hour: he shot past rifles
twisted like Chesterfield spires,
body snatchers, toffee-apples,
cakes of chestnut on the slabs
of dead trees, into a shell-hole, sleep.

Jack wakes, follows his boots straight
into enemy lines. Cake Day it

is not: they give him pieces of
their Prussian minds; his cake-hole, fist-fulls
until they feast the Madiera,
eat your cake and save your dough.

Yorkshires bloom in the oven like clouds
as I dicker with citron, sack,
rose-water for a tansy-cake:
it's hogmanay in my kitchen,
flooded with light and mixing bowls,
darkening with a switch to Jack.

Charlie and Sassoon

'But where was the glory for the obscure private?'
— SIEGFRIED SASSOON, *Complete Memoirs of George Sherston*

'For muddy boots, we had our recommendation quashed.'
— CHARLES ROWLAND, *unpublished memoirs of World War One*

Cumbered with trench mouth in the potting-mould,
Sassoon, with muddy eyes, matchsticks for eyes
among the scrooping trenchboards and swiped graves,
thinks of ideas running out of soldiers,
privates that spoke as they found, and fell where they lay
—No Man's Land no longer powdered with rain
and the drabs in the gather back home—
teaches new lads how to survive, not win,
useful as the basket of homing pigeons
ejected from planes if you landed in the drink.

Private without clover in a flea-bag,
your mouth tastes of railways as you detrain,
mouthing absent goodbyes to girls dragging
ploomed white feathers for spurred recruits
at Leeds Central Station. For Kangar (Sassoon),
breezes ruffle the reedy French pools,
an Acq shepherd tootles, the trees frou-frou,
thinking of salpiglossis; whereas you
tend the sanies from the privates' ulcers
all Heath Robinson without a servant's say-so.

Both knew it was war from the mushroom flush
in Morlancourt—unpicked—and the cricket
strips without explosive shots or slips.
Your words are like fish out of meadow rush.
Chas versus Sassoon's cowls of hop-kilns
means nothing in the context of his
memoirs of the flooded cemetery.

Can I dad this? I remember your hand,
Christmas trees over Dresden, the black
bacteria of photographs. And that is . . .
memory. A slab of difficult memory.

The Long Cyclops
i.m. Charles Rowland, 1896–1982

Never such Crab Nebulae again
above an earth as viscous as butter.
All humpy knapsack, the family's milk-tooth,
you fear your ante-bellum hours
are baking as fast as a Pudding Lane.
Surrounded by your head in the army barbers,
you remember Evelyn's kiss but must feel
no more than a rock. Scarborough breaks
as precious as loaves. Duck boards. Sump holes.
Your mouth in your heart on the parapet.

Floored only by cowpox you dream
of *Fricholompsis rutilans*, the plum
and custard mushrooms of Woodhouse Ridge.
The fool's bolt is soon shot, so you catch
your death o' cold among the puggarees
of abandoned ridges. You talk to your own worms
and ghost, carry the moon with you
across a No Man's Land of Venus
minus trees, thinking of the biscuits
bricked in tins, then stewed in tea.
The French retreat from your Whippet tank,
leaving you henned with a Lee-Enfield,
cooped beyond *kleos*. Beyond your long Cyclops,
you butcher at trenches of Willi Wakkers.

Far from the pampelmousse of the Marais,
but with secret wells of yoghurt in your mind,
you enfilade. Eyebrows tumble.
A trench is gained. You leave a trench coat
in your cellar—so heavy it props
like a lead tepee—where your children play
doctors and the garden waits.
They twist a flower under your jaw
to betray its love of butter.
Your face opens like the right clover.

Cucumber

'Why cucumber sandwiches?'
               — OSCAR WILDE, *The Importance of Being Earnest*

Indigestion circles harm the salad, *Cucurbitacaeae*,
Asia's creeping plant, bitter herbis, dry as a stick
to Wyclif and his cucumeris that waxen in exotic lands,
obscene in the fridge, yellow and long—the cowcumber,
lovely bruised juice of the leaves, uncookable
tender annual from 1573 in this country
from the East Indies, commonly eaten as a cooling salad
or pickling, burping cucumbers in Virgil
among the surface creep, hard as stones,
with crooked bodies and with bellies deep, the
bellying cucumber, cucumber-cool, cucumber-time,
the tailors' holiday ('Here a scratch, there a scritch,
Cucumber, Cucumber ho!'), this cross-legg'd
cabbage-eating son of a porn cucumber,
bitter cucumber, suckling cucumber, one-seeded,
single-seeded or star cucumber, serpent or
snake-cucumber, spirting or squirting cucumber
—the fruit of which when ripe separates from the stalk
and blurts the seeds and pulp with considerable force
and was favoured by Venetian architects,
who gobbled the green microphone
like a winter warmer, wet minstrel, a tune
('Exterminate the pippy fuckers!'),
rich man's raddichio, abominable lolly, a sick green cigar,
perverted ice pop, goblin-coloured slime merchant,
fruit-lather at the lips like dog-froth, canal water
plapping to the courtier chomp ('Which idiot let this in?')—
leapyng cucumber, Pulp of Coloquintida, Viper Gourd,
Big Burpless Hybrids, oriental trellis cuke farmers
frequently six or more feet long, and at first striped
with different shades of green, porraceous
Mrs Mitford—'He ... made a very decent cucumber-bed

in mine host's garden'—and Dr Johnson's advice: cucumber should always be well sliced, dressed with pepper and vinegar, and then be slung out, as good for nothing.

Cwm

What cuckoos say you know
as we pocket throatwort,
sneezewort and baby's breath
to ward off your first illness
clean as a whitewashed crease.

You point towards the cwm,
its katabatic scree;
frapple your own shadow
as the sun's magnesium
lamps the mustard fields.

You sigh your heart-sluffs
but please do not eat your shoes
as we dummy the Ross Cobb
chicken sheds, hock burns surrounded
with oilseed, brassica and charlock.

Condemned to smile in the park,
we patrol the mini-coaches
until the gulls' dives spoke us home:
we pad the landing carpet
to eye-glitter in the dark cot.

We turn on the mortalities
downstairs and the news-gluts on
'conventional' bombs, survivors
mobbed with question marks, an open bus
in conventional air.

Ox

Naked as the dawn with a parsnip eyebrow
our baby moons herself and lolls my sleeve; razzes, hoots,
makes me feel as useless as a Picston Shottle,
hockles the last instruction as milk water plocks
in the kitchen with memories of butterscotch
Angel Delight, hash fritters like moons with butter-pocks,
the pornography of sild and cold tongue lathered
in greaseproof that gran boxed by cellophane Lamberts.

Primped and snoggled for Bolling Hall and its headless
Roundhead, she nevertheless doubled with liver pain
as the black ox trod on your crimping toes
on the Sticker Lane pavement into a dream-ghost
not quite visible and yet not quite unknown.
Tomorrow, after custard, I'll be served skin.

Rain-pie

'[A child] may get on his mother's nerves with the awkward
problem why a bench is called a bench'
— Theodor Adorno

Chomping on the buffets like bench-whistlers,
our starfishes tending to the bench-hole,
I muse on the benk and the bink,
locals who busked to the 'benke Where baneres are bright'
and the bench-warmers who loved 'The summer binks,
a benched alcove or summer-house'. Benk, bink:
northern words usurped by German benchmarks.

Why was my mother threng, not busy with the pots,
and why did she chump when my father progged,
collecting wood for Bonfire Night?
Etymological stories lost in the epic drive
between Frizinghall and Sticker Lane, Laisterdyke.
When I exclaimed, seven, 'There's a yak on the bench!',
there was no need to coin the laughing cuff.

Last Easter broke like a podge of cream
(binks of emetic eggs, of Yorkie chickens)
and Akil, seven, spelt as he found, a hanger in his hair,
spitting 'Where's the buffalo?' for buffet,
and the roast flowed with the steam of potatoes
and something was dissing with the lilac tree
after the winter, after the crash.

Bank Holiday and a drouth of rain-spatter
for your father's blood oranges and barbecue.
Apart, we never glozed on each other, remained
the lexical space between chiton and chitterling,
k'wai k'wai and chop-chop. Chop-chop
on the news, the butchers in Zimbabwe,
the gulf from Rhodesia, Sierra Leone.

And so I celebrate the distance
between Akil, his dreads and the hanger,
colonialism, Mugabe, white farmers,
and contemplate a Kleftiko;
I long for hot cross buns, not pink drumsticks
and the fry of your late winter warmer.
Why is a bench not a buffet, a tuffet or spread?

April peace in the rhythm of cyclometers
and the thresh of the beach of night:
our evenings may have been smidgens of smackeroos
as we tested, after moving, the benks in our bond
but we were never ham or eggs, nor chalk or cheese;
instead, we remainder, moraine, as rare as the bridge
between rain-pie and peewit, woodpecker and lapwing.

The Flies' Cemetery

'Our slubbers have not given over feasting yet: they have done
nothing these three days past: they are a set of clever fellows'
— '*The Diary of Joseph Rogerson, Scribbling Miller of Bramley, 1808–1814*'

Bring me luscious comestibles: I shall
make myself whole again with a Lambswool bowl,
poultry from the butter-cross and moulded Tipsy cake,
December fruit, Morley tusky, *Rheum rhaponticum*,
garden rhubarb with Yorkshire relish that makes
the plainest viands — like you — palatable
with black treacle, vinegar and spice. Eat not to dullness.
Beware of a silent dog and still water, snow cakes
when not a haddock stands in the fields. Desire
for sweet grape-coffins comes from the water-pudding,
the spoon stooked in the porridge, clapcake faces
round the scoured table and spicket-pot, manchet
in the broth for us greasy slubbers, whereas you
conduct cattle droves through our town with clowns
I cannot understand, circus menageries
with hairless horses, without the fear of liver
and whitewash week. We must throw pussy willow
in Howley water for its healing powers after
spinning the trencher, kissing through chairs,
slope back to our onions ('working-man's beef')
goat the bread and cheese of hawthorn roots, aching
for skull-draggers, steaks with oatcakes dripped in blood;
your blood. An apple pie without the cheese is like
a kiss without the squeeze. First time this season
I have noticed apples crying. I digress;
think of you in a Vulcan fat press, or potato
beaten with dripping during the dripping riot,
imagine spreading dripping on your dripping crimson
Brussels carpet, alpaca curtains, Spanish sideboard,
cutting cut glass in your perfect little bijou
as you gorge in the town hall on *Potage Crème d'Orge*.

Over-crusted windows sugar the Plot night.
Through the fingers of my mind I see you pick
on *Baba à la Polonaise, Whitebait Diable,*
my sour grapes crumbing your Utrecht velvet, always
on the wrong side of your favourite dumb waiter.

1926
i.m. Tom Rowland, 1915–2001

You tweeze nuggets from the clinker
with the same delicacy
as you twist a rose's stem, as if
it distilled mineral, or pistils
that might bouquet any moment
like the flowers of coal among the slag.

Your roses are sickening. A dream of beef
means the death of a friend or relative
when you pore over cod, swimming in parsley.
You can train a cat into a hedge
but Mischief Night trims your evergreens
into privet ribbons, felines into Manx.

You wish you could guddle their bangers,
as poisonous as ragwort no topiary
can heal. The spangles of frost
slacken on an irretrievable hedge.
I cannot bear your garden, only
those round shoulders that now are mine.

You lose your sea-legs among the clinkers
of rose hips, sway among the moon-pennies,
the ox-eye daisies, as your throat slackens,
your heart slows to the pace of the moor,
an Elysium of dingles, arrowroot biscuits,
the rose of Jericho, and all privets intact.

On my wrist, you tick me off. 'Clown!'
The smatters of ice pile like grit,
ichthyoid on this, your final Friday,
which was always the fishmonger's.
The sun pokes through a glassy morning.
The thaw-wind pothers round the chimney slack.

Ganton Mount
i.m. Willie Rowland, 1878–1941

The silent moon tiptoes the night as you
outstare the clock, each other, the porridge
of family love, care-worn stubbornness.

Addressing the stone in the cottage,
the plaster a canvas for your hatreds,
you wrestle to recall you are brothers

since Willie took London as his patron,
dreamed himself cuts above the northern goose
at the Rowland table, his own apron-strings

and tenement heretics, quit the house
for young Lily's allotments and snickets;
leg-tailed it back, when she died, to roost.

The pan-hand at a brushmakers, polished
bowlers, rolled umbrella, velvet and spats
offend Harry with his wax moustache,

cleaning apron and fastidiousness:
Will wrapped clunkers of coal in newspaper,
cursed the dust-webs' scatter round the scuttle-grit.

Victorian men check the time with no face
as I pootle through their absent streets,
Leeds window-grimace of fresh milkshakes.

Trees' bones settle round the living-room feet
while you graze in each others' eyes like cats,
keep the terrace buttoned, go out into sleet.

Mistle from 1900

On Woodhouse Ridge, the hills are still
quilted with flowing stone. Below,
William Rowland rivets shoes for life.
Astronauts are ghosts
clumping his mind where money burns
and motorways din to its cusp.

It is 1896.
A keen frost sips at the veins.
He sits on a roof of a school,
pooling his lenses for Jupiter's moons.
Sanded all winter, they are darkly poised.

There is the hand of a dead man on my bookshelf:
his letters shiver on a yellow sheet.
I am thumbing his son's indentures.
He cleaves me with a century,
years of stars, light years younger.

My grandad is a twinkle.
His love was plants, not planets.
I see him bellamy through rubber leaves
preening the edges for the pith of thrips.

In the year of the thrush,
William's prize glass hairlines.
His head whites overnight
but he remains aloft,
only days away from the grave,
imbibing cobblers to astral clusters.

Pomfret
i.m. Thomas Rowland, 1915–2001

During the ides of pyres of feet and mouths,
your joints are cooling in the living room.
You leave in your last ambulance and then
the calm in the departed house is colossal;
I wait on your doorstep, and meet a door.

The wake candles your home with relatives:
an aunt is on the fritz with an affidavit
for a teapot which hints at your wrists.
Some saw you as a gimmer with a fat sandwich,
evenings measured with fig biscuits
as your thews drew closer to hospital beds.

I see your coffin of my mind and cross
memories part up Barkerend Road:
the shock of your box amongst traffic.

Those little cakes of Pontefract not fish
are unnibbled beside the curtailed shopping list;
sweet meat accompanies the easing of your pulse.

Our last conversation was of dripping:
your laughter and cooking an antidote
to an empty home and calendar,
save 'library', 'library', and 'hair'.

Cromwell's Toothbrush

Politics has powdered down to mulletgate,
the Low Sunday in Hay, Haie, *Y-Gelli*, 'Grove'
of jumbo eggs and oven-ready geese.
Pages of verdigris await our baited eyes
above the moat of road. We plunder
the patchouli rooms, obscure sooterkins
of second-hand bookshops, slim volumes
selling like lukecakes. Biographies are snapped;
whereas, up in the alcoves, History moulds.
Long-lost novels greet us like lovers, just out of reach.

Touch the spines of the Wildlife section:
Crepidula fornicata, the clothes of the slipper
limpet and mitten crabs; saury—a long-beaked fish
from *sauros*, the horse-mackerel. See the moya,
the volcanic mud in the Geography section;
moulins, the fissures in glaciers; the metempsychosis
of squirrels; our blackthorn winter,
when blossom freezes on the branches of March.

We are neonates in this place with wrong questions on our lips:
Is Cromwell's toothbrush before Worcester historical or not?
The hunch of backs is a Rump Parliament in the snug
as we clap our eye-beams on gammon in The Lion,
mock-Commonwealth candles and goode beer,
which is good and converts me to a one-pint screamer.
These Landlords are the prayer books of our gossipy age:
we are party to the fact that a jill is a ferret, not a measure,
from a man who looks like my father,
whose eloquence with wood embarrasses
my inarticulacy with banisters; tyres with kerb rash.
His eye is a spirit level and it accuses.

I pretend to listen to a carpet which croons behind a settee,
turns into a rather persuasive collie.

The piped musak is the will to content the people,
given up long ago for mobile phones.
We earwig those who come in with the milk bottles,
kettled, trollied, mullered, muppets who were clangered
with mutts, mucky ducks and swamp donkeys.

In the same plot of sky:
the vatic sun, the inviolable moon.
We luff our silhouettes from the avenue of eggs,
our thoughts leaving for our murine kitchen at home:
its furry secret beats under the fridge.
As Oestre's hares pick the hills,
we quit The Lion with its eyes on the walls,
shadowed by Offa, Wye and its dykes,
the gentle rays of Hay fleeing our lids.

Primigravida

Venice's water-slap and plastic bobs
dissolve lagoons into Ruskin's sugar,
stopper the enclosures like durians.
We contribute our own plastics
for horse noodles in frothy markets.
San Marco's misshapen pearls float
tokens of your reflection by the Molo,
as your tip-toes ripple the womb.
Ripped off with a cake near the Bridge of Sighs,
the Campanile watches us take five
as our antler-glasses prevent a peck
by the Procuratie Vecchie,
hawked by the bags and gondolier sticks
like barbers' poles, Arabian ogives.

Walls offend Ruskin with their deadness:
by any stretch, we cannot smooth
our mixed cheeks onto your absent face,
small ghost in the sand of the C.T.G.
If the most beautiful things in the world
are the most useless, you are a peacock
or the lilies in the Dent du Midi.
In the Castelvecchio galleries,
a baby offers us a chaffinch,
voiding at the cynosure.
A Veronese zealot has chipped
the *Tacuinum sanitatis*:
the due amanti always miss
their dill, starch, wine and kiss.

A man aims a telephone at himself,
smiles, and pockets the future;
our breather. The sea and sky patter:
rain melts into glacial water
as your eyes start to bloom

and your stomach feathers. Statues
wake the children in the museum
as we settle for prosecco,
astronomical gelatino.
A vaporetta's wake jellies
and your head nudges the fundus.
Far from the peanuts, the grain
of St. Mark's Square and tweenie hats,
your first movements bubble.

Polly

Your gift of poppy-juice,
meconium, windy smile,
little clutch at the wind-shift
of cars outside the lampshade.
Scissors are an open blackbird.
The coble basket pots your dreams
and brussen cheeks, beautiful
white meat. Give us thick ears
for inattention, try your muscles,
your run of faces, listen to
the trees' music, changes of light
between rooms; panic at rubber limbs
under the raw moon, broad
sunshine and resistance in pockets
on the news. A child smokes in school.
'Give me an apple', he says
as he expands from the wreckage.

The Land of Green Ginger

My grandad preserves Mothers' Day cards
from the year my grandma died
whereas I saw an ex in an open coffin
(tripping by the law courts in The Land of Green Ginger)
and, smiling at her first question,
('Are we going to touch hands all night?')
by the weeping fat in The Bun in the Oven.

Three quarters of a strawberry, orange juice and sleep,
the tab left me sipping her traces.
Passion cake crumped on the tongue.
There were two views in one window,
the floor sloped doorwards in pinks and blues,
the bath and loo were a picture
and I glooped on the rim where her hairs rippled.

Outside was too much.
The green man gave me the runs
as pigeons crossed the morning streets.
Back home in the garden,
crumbs wormed on a chopping board
and as sheets shivered in the acid wind,
I let out loaves for the early birds.

Cech Speaks

I name a hill a mountain. Ríp.
I consult my map. It is blank (apart from Ríp)
so I name a stream after my elbow
and the land after myself.
Lech forks north and founds Poland.
He cannot face three-word I-Spy,
or years of Smâzény syr.

Wenceslas, neither king nor good,
crisps a snowball with the tongues
of St Vitas's gargoyles in his sights.
Terezín bleeds afresh 'ARBEIT MACHT FREI'.
Tanks pock the National Museum,
shells smack a raspberry surface
that hides marble, not the parliament.

Stâre Mésto could be St Michael's Mount,
were it not for the villa's facade,
which crumbles behind state perfection
to a rot of sump and public toilets.
Guards slurp in a hut lapped by the Vltava,
waiting with sandwiches for Vaclav Haval.
Ice cream cones flash in Wenceslas Square.

Golem

We come from beyond the Slovak pail
to find snails on nippy streets
the Sunday rain washed the Vltava plain.
A cat roils a washing line with drops
watching us pale from the CSA plane.
A dog nips at our shadows, barking for sun
and the balmy simplicity of Czech afternoons
but it is as warm as when Rabbi Löw glued
his golem together from Vltava turf.

With you in a pivnice, chilled by wine
bubbling with the graves of Vyšehrad
engraved in your camera, a tomb
for the embarrassment of tourists.
You long for foxes in the Southern Cemetery,
not the thin, spooky statues heavening here.
Your arm gooses when I brush it
by a mausoleum, your lilac smile
like light frosted on the white walls.

We sit like fish as a street boy slips
a backpacker's bag from a Coke café.
The velvet revolution is a trail
of brown amok in our red and white cups.
As we eat ice cream in Wenceslas Square
(neither square, nor good),
Russian bears pause in the National Museum,
frozen in a language I can barely understand.
Take my hand. Feel the sundae heat.

Terezín

New York arose from a tulip; Prague
from Václav Klaus's tightrope to the market
not good Libuše's prophesy that Krok
and his threshold city would reach the stars.
Stag nights mingle on the statues' oches
crunched by succession and Vltava flows.
The newly caked buildings ruin Koprova
with its bursting markets, a balloon tree, knedlícky,
Terezín ruins, Beth Chaim ('the House of Life'),
pebbled in with the dead wood and squeezing graves.

Dawn crawls with flowers
that last longer than boys;
the streets, open cloacas, in březen,
the birch month. Garrets scream
with light, coffee-coloured plates,
the shame clots. At night, the girls
dream of sleep in carbolic air.
Dandelions with heavy foreheads
and the chestnuts white like candles.

Cherubs winkle the blackened sermons
that discombobulated Protestant heads
on Charles Bridge rippled with steady cameras.
The parting of the years settles
on St. Joachim who gives a finger
to the Stalin monument, now absent
during prosinec, season of the slaughtered, and
the daffodil revolution in Kyrgyzstan.

Rowland on the Hair

'The true secret of British superiority lies in ... a barber's basin'
— ALEXANDER ROWLAND, 1853

Noiseless muttonchops like the great institutions
repel these blasphemies against the face
such as the shorn Neopolitan dandies
currently trembling the Italian State.
Envious Indians have a terror of wigs
and the Easter Island natives, of our whiskers:
they have no barbers, but neighbourly kindness prevails,
whereas English beards are the cleanest things that sail.

Sadly, King Arthur's beard is dead and the queues
in Guiana are breathlessly obese.
Southey said if he had a beard he would cherish it
for his pleasure, regale it on a summer's day,
offer incense with a pastille, sugar and lavender;
advised all Britons to desist from pollarding
the face peduncle since the man with facial equipment
does not bend to anyone and the tooth-ache too
has been dismissed by a perspicuous thatch.

Rome was sacked by the barbarous, shaven Gauls
then William Nelsoned the English to the strop
and French: we all left at that point for the azure main
and saw Mongolian hair cast by the Ganges
and Mount Beloor; the woolly hair of Barbary women
(who nevertheless are tolerably handsome)
and the Arnos who have beards liked kites. Dr Latham doubts this
as well as the laughable anecdote of an African fop.
Orientals always take care of their beards
unlike the undulated Bedouins Arabs think fabulous.
Chinese women are allowed to wear cabbages.
Egyptians dress their nails with privet leaves and the Japanese
resemble a four-cornered piece of japanned wood.

Every shore of the enslaved encircles ours.
Japanese hairdressers are really good.

Oleaginous Melacoshimans with kaame-saashee
and oosee-dashee ornaments are similar
to the people of Loo-choo. For the Bishareens,
ghee is ineffectual against vermin
and the false locks of Nigritian beauties.
Esqimaux women who chop are disgraceful
and doomed to eternal celibacy.
In the Sandwich Islands, the hair is rather coarse
and has not that gloss of an English lady's horse.

And I remember the dark angels of Australia
decorated with opossum and kangaroo,
the Egyptian beauties dripping with castor oil,
typee damsels and their attention to their tresses,
as well as rosin, bread-fruit, and Polynesian mouoi.
Enough, of fashionable hairdressing in the African desert.
Our civilised chins shall once again repose
in the oaky shadow of perennial pilosity,
and our barbers, repelling the tyrannical hoardes,
shall be restored to pristine dignity
as the cultivator of man's distinguishing appendage.

Lésvos

The candles only make us see the dark
more clearly, a nightmare head
clapped by the shuttles.
Spoondrift lovers spoon by the wind's edge
where Orpheus's skull
lolled around inlets, rosy fingers
as dextrous as pilliwinks
in the torturous sun.

A Turkish minaret piggybacks
Greek Molyvos, spoon-baits
through the rock to the mackerel.
An Orthodox congregation
slowpokes to the church,
past these strung octopi,
salting Mussolinis,
the wind-chimes of unseen kri-kri.

We gentoo seaward,
as if at an absent ship or the breeze
that colours the wheat.
Gull-roosts dribble the Aegean,
the dipping mist. Swallows collect.
I have not found you again and you
are closer to the Styx than a skimmed pebble.
The sun hods the sky, the armies of nimbus.

Skála Eressou

This is a lesbian-only resort:
quickly, queer the beach. Would Orpheus,
who loved the loúloudha of tender men,
be banned from crawling
the pools' electric currents; straight-only hotels?
Our eyes run to fat on our stomachs,
our proprietor's Sapphic wit: fish
in Lesbian sauce at The Tenth Muse.

Bogue
i.m. Tom Rowland, 1915–2001

'Hello! At last you have found me!'
     — SIGN, ÁNAXOS TAVERNA

The old moon lies in the new moon's arms
above this last resort: I look for you
among derricks and abandoned lido.
The throngs of less distinguished dead
twitter like bats in Asphodel Fields.
I think of the Maunder Minimum,
while Menos pulls the rock from under our feet
all night, and the porgy in the bay
are calmed by the first quarter of sky.
Your blank postcard stares up with a bogue's eye.

'Don't touch me when I'm going down things.'
I picture a man with his hands in your chest.
After the op., you were what you ate:
pinkness of carotene as if from shrimp,
diatom or carrots. One lung, not leg.
My mooning catches me like the lamellae
in this pat of Kallonˊı flamingos,
ghosts of the Egyptian sun god.
You have left for more than a furlough.
You are my hypogeum.

'Do not through the paper' to Lethe.
O Kipos, Mary, if only you had known
the impossibility of not meeting tourists.
Two donkeys eeyore outside
Pigassus pizzas with pizza 'for tow'
instead of spanokópites and tyrópites.
The fingers of Helios, fallen through clouds
to Lesbos, this island of the son of the sun,
shine on the lizards that shed their towels,
and the conga of cars towards the beach.

I hope your island of the Blest, not Asphodel,
lies under the stick of this boat to Skaminía
and a vocabulary of stars, your neap
still crusted on our legs tomorrow
and the tentacles like clothes
that dry on the lines of Tsónia.
Son of your son, you skirt my dreams
like the martin that nips the Aegean
to swallow. I cannot swallow your death
until I find your horizontal line in my head.

Io

Even as a cow you are lovely.
Paradise lies just around the corner
where muscles toffee and calves elasticate:
not the clouds that laze over Ithaca
or the sparkle of waves, Cephallonian blue,
but a beach in Ayía Efimía,
pebbled with tennis balls of sea urchins,
nobs yammering with spiky feet,
squid lips in forty-degree rays.
We wake up and flee from ourselves.

'Did you like your chair last night?'
I overhear my own converse
within a cooee of your closed ears
as the commerce of Fiskárdho
blurs around us. Our menu tonight
is not prepared with the words we relish
(melitzanosaláta, horiátiki,
kopanistí, papoutsákia, karpoúzi),
but special intestines, drunkman's platter, nests and zombies.
I rumble and confuse you for a sleek heifer.

'How can you associate a few
unsuspecting bats with death?'
nobbles the guide to Melissáni,
cave of the nymphs, where Homer
says the bees nest. Next day
we peer into the mouth of a cavern
where Germans were sacked from a U-boat,
mutilated among Pan's horn of plenty,
the echo of these stalagmites.

Watermelon entrails and bouzouki
on Daskaliá, where the suitors sharpened
their tongues before losing them,
waiting for Odysseus, chomping
on the honey-cake of Penelope.
Mythical food tastes best: arbute berries,
combs from the holm-oak; only
rovaní with ice cream in Ithaki comes close;
spoons licked on a verandah
among the rain of shooting stars.

'Please do not step on the fridge.' You low
about the impossibility of not being a tourist.
So, for once I relax at the yachts,
the bougainvillaea, the chichi,
the bon ton of catamarans. The chariot
of the sun melts across the harbour
as we wait for the horn of the moon.
Flags ripple in the zephyr as red
as these irises with letters on their petals
that spell 'AI AI' (alas, alas).

Gently Michael
i.m. Mike Holt, 1954–2004

A plane silvers the pink
above the garden's tacky plaques
on the clipped lawn where we long-grass,
among the spinners, our grief
this crisp afternoon. No curtain,
but today you will be burnt
as our suits drip-mould the service,
the congregation lowers
its chin music for the flowers,
Mahler and the bored organist,
vulpine ash catkins at the back.
The sky has gone; the cloud-hanks.
Swallows gem the lines and a child
lets a balloon into bitter night.

Chestnut Avenue

The morning toothbrush comes too soon
after the evening moved from caribou to carobs,
and the way your chutney looks like chyme.
Our talk cut short by the kettle's skittling,

I wrinkled in its surface, my cheeks perfected back,
face slack with tea-steam and tears for Sunday,
the glare of kisses in forecourts, a shame
the lines are unhindered with leaves or snow.

Back home, my yukka laps the draught.
Chestnuts butt the flue with feathered fruit.
Galey with rain, sycamores lisp.
The leaves brush with your fingertips.

Tongue and Udder

Staring at a diagram of a cow,
I recall our sojourns, your fatty hands
on my aitch bone and chuck; mine, on your clod
or shol, Sir Loin or veiny piece. Peace.
I must ragout all parts of the animal, from
collared pig's face to the fricass'd calf's feet.
Like Mrs Raffald's Hare, you send me
to the Table, lay me with Sippets
but take out the onion at the Kings Head
in Salford; indulge in the orange cream
of my untrembling thighs, your face as lithe
as a Yarmouth bloater, your lips larded
like a poulard, green goose or shivered ox palates.
You shuffle to a pottle of strawberries ripe
for their gill and aristocratic salad.
Tonight, I shall dandle a trussed woodcock
for your buds, tease them with the sate
of chardoons with cheese. I do not do
the colly-flower. Steam your desire
with a hot Cheese-Iron or crimp cod with flour.
Chrysanths will get you nowhere, or salmagundy.
Perhaps, *ce soir*, you might care for *torrent de veau*,
pulpeton, *matelot* of tame duck, beef *tremblong*, Larks
à la Surprise, *petit* pigeons, fillets of soals
but if you want French cooks you must have French tricks.
Adams Luxury, and Eve's Cookery
demands that we 'should always look cool,
inviting and dainty'; or was that the Pease?
My dream is to pickle flowers at dawn
in gally pots or double glass, covered
with your bladder; bruised and the juice drawn
with a simmer. If your teeth asketh,
suck on marigolds, or peck of cowslips.
Lately, a poodle has answered to your thigh:
lovingly, 'For the Biting of a Mad Dog'

I prepare the broth of Primrose roots stamped
in white wine and strained with something else.
Let the patient drink a good draught of it.

Moose

In Piscataquis county, north-west Maine, numerous place names contain the word 'moose' or 'squaw'. In spring 2002, the local council decided that, due to the fact that 'squaw' is considered to be offensive by some native Americans, the relevant places would have to be renamed. Unfortunately, the word chosen to replace 'squaw' was 'moose'
— article in *The Guardian*

Would it be barking up the wrong poodle, sir,
to suggest that the proliferation of moose
might damage the economy of the Passamaquoddy?
Tourists will shake their heads,
bamboozled by signs for Moosehead,
Moose Bay, Moose Brook, Little Moose Brook,
Little Moose Pond, Big Moose Pond, Big Moose Mountain,
Little Moose Township, Moose Point and Mount Moose Bosom.
Us Piscataquis will continue to call a squaw a squaw.
For what are we supposed to do with the mousse?
Is there a squaw in the fridge?
Give me a gob iron to break the Maine rule
in the key of C with the song of the moose
who left me, took a train to Chicago,
where the bog pans are as huge as a moose's flank.
The night draws breath as I utter a squaw.
Chose a lifestyle as steady as a trivet, she did,
instead of putting pegs on everything, as she did,
escaped from the absence of the name she hated,
from *otsíkwaw*, the holiest of holies, prostitute,
that lead the Penobscot tribe to replace
White Squaw Island with No Name Island.
Now, under the moon I confuse for a moose,
I sing the blues about all loose moose, of how
I need your nameless body more than you do.

Press-ganged

The queen waves to brains on the starboard,
the blood washed away with officers' paint.
Cannons ricochet to the dead among decks
without legs. Exsanguination:
our torsos were treble-shotted,
a clown ripped from the stage in Cadiz,
the drift of fibreglass yachts.
History pageantry or carnage party:
is this a review or revision?

Old foes celebrate the sea's friendship
with mega-firework fleet illumination,
whereas we have dined with Duke Humphrey,
bitten by a barnmouse, kisky,
smelling of cork—a brick in the hat—
jug-bitten by the brewer's horse,
nuzzled with a drop of sun in the eye,
pontooned, to forget; but I can still just
taste the sparrow-grass and sea-dust.

That summer of blood and laughter,
seaborn assaults near St Mère-Eglise
and Pegasus Bridge, ten thousand
lost on somebody's birthday.
War memorials stake the villages
with lachrymatory sunflower fields.
Skrimshankers on the beach are left with half-
forgotten memories of les enfants,
shaved women to assuage other guilts.

R.A.F. Mapless

'With our equipment we can track a broom in space'
— FYLINGDALES

They think we are Russian,
are not suckered by 'us' boar, 'mi' owl
and flippers ground at Headingley,
but we were taken in by the roundels
burnt on the tarmac of absent children,
surrounding a classroom
cordoned with airstrips.

I want Brownie points for History,
but they believe we are briefed,
know the exact location and range
of Fylingdales, the ack-acks at Spurn
and the bunkers grassed at Dane's Dyke,
so they exception to the camera
swept up by surveillance, and ask us inside.

The school is not a school.
A lift clinks shut; its cables tick
through tunnels mushroomed with warheads.
Double exposed, we are dusted
into a mirage of blue heat and home,
waiting for the knocks, the bristle of feet,
and the collage of limbs and brooms in the cupboard.

I.M. Deltics, 1977–81

Nothing compares to the smooth curve of windows
and six cylinders beneath bolted blue.
Shunting up behind me, their breath steams,
pistons pump against the metal sweating blebs,
I shut my notebook and go home to bed.

I cried when they scrapped that class.
They guillotined The Earl of Westmoreland's rear,
his spent grease guttered across the sweltering yard.
Now I dream of flying over humming sheds
and oiling engines, worrying whether it's correct
to scribble them down without being whole.

On the platform of awful pies,
buttocks ribbed on a pack-up seat,
I flask and muse, what if stars aren't stars,
but holes in black bodywork through
to a blaze of whistles where 55s go?

London Particular

'It is at the next doore on both hands of mee, and under
the same roofe.'
—John Allin, 1665

'No more sullen beast than a he drab'
behind the pub's sooty vestiture.
A London particular
flumes the streets like blood.

Legs of brittle children
hoisted as faggots
rack past the window, snitched
from the bone cart.

Sixpence for a kinch
from Pardon Churchyard
or noyous Houndsditch.
Steeping the roofes, behind daubed doors:

the fumes and miasma
of the jolted. 'Faggots, faggots!'
A stiffness lobes my ear;
a swelling will not rise or break.

Philtres before the choacking.
Mountebanks dispense
treacles, cordials,
fulvous plague waters.

Every drab for himself
with a hanged-skull cure,
a dead handshake or
the spoonwort of scurvy quacks.

All us punks, doxies and smuts
trugmoldies, punchable nuns,
blowzes and buttered buns,
who glub in The Pye,

in for a fuddle or a nip,
seal abracadabra
in our pockets, an amulet
against the offal pits,

'continuall ringing
and tolling of bells',
Feare and Trembling—
the Catch-Polles of Death.

Clouds of sea-coal
ring both hands of mee,
the greasy puddles
of Wilderness Row,

riffled by the cat's-paw,
sun-gash. Catarrhal mists
lap my steps, the detritus
by the Fleet of a mud-lark.

'Green you bugger, why don't you fire?'
Gasp among the pea-souper,
charlock, broad dock and sun spurge.
The evening sets heliotropic cobs.

Suffrage
i.m. Harry Rowland, 1880–1953

I.

In 1911,
George Harrison & Sons,
Hammerton Street, burned.

A petrol can legerdemain,
suspected suffragettes
from Back Lane.

Before Emily Davison
and for Emmeline Pankhurst,
the torch.

Her mind a racecourse,
the anonymous who kissed
the Georges with flame.

Lame presses and printers
crickled in Fahrenheit,
faradic in heat.

Footleberry girls
were prickling as bricks
bulged like bog spavins and dropped.

The building a church,
hiss of suffrage,
intercessory petition.

It shook like a lamb,
came to its knees,
gave in to rubble, history.

II.

The rafters bounced down
like a table after cockle-bread,
Guy Forks burs.

Having raised to a fare-you-well,
the crisps of women
back, farouche, slunk.

Storming of printers
not a parliament
did not settle Emmeline.

Until the parody of Aintree,
horse, damages,
vote, professions.

Plattons licked in their ink,
Cylinders withholding
print of tomorrow.

A buckshee of paper
was futtering with vim
to the warming soil.

The muted boxes of type
slid through split boards
like a cran of herring.

A machine man,
my great grandfather an effigy
as his trade slipped.

III.

As his bestest Cylinder
flushed like a Tipler
into the basement.

The air a farrago of ash
Ellen Rowland held,
fiercely stare.

To Percy Lund Humphries
after Otley called George
where he slunk with sons.

Where, fifty years later,
my dad apprenticed,
approved with indentures.

Harry lit the gas flame
during his apprenticeship
at Briggate dawns.

In Nelsen's yard, a race
for meetings at Wetherby
Doncaster, York.

The listings were grasped
by the Leeds Central bookies
for Pontefract nags.

Due for a full wage, sacked.
Then Tapp & Toothills,
Bramley, Pudsey, Bradford.

IV.

A myth he commuted
miles each day
by foggy foot to Canal Road.

Evening fish
and chips he delivered in baskets
from future Bryans.

Egg baps and barms
while the Parish's graveyard,
soon cathedral, was dug.

Lives reduced to witnesses:
Inman and Gibson
at St George's Church.

Married with Dorrie
and early upsets, Ellen
took prams to Thetford.

Whooping killed Dorrie
at three. Then Plimsoll Street
where the roof-plaster coughed.

After the fire,
Legrams Lane for die,
then litho and letterpress.

BDA let him lie
for Bottomleys, uncontrolled heat,
paper-stretch.

v.

Setting type, he cast
his own rollers, used wood
to prove that the walls bulged.

Cobbled shoes.
Ellen fried breakfasts
up at the crack, then back for dinner.

Baking day.
My grandad remembers pies,
bread and pastries laid to cool.

Hammerton then a shed
of shunters we twitched
for elusive 01s.

But these are loops of blank ems:
we cannot find our selves
in relatives.

There is no quiddity
even in the ones we know,
not the rested.

So. St James. Au bord
to rusted 03s
where I ate dream sandwiches.

Three months of wrongly
splet graffiti, a hose
that snaked, would not go off.

VI.

I swept the market
with milk-bottle toilets
for those who used their hands.

We played overs
with planks and aubergines,
dreaming of Pudsey St Lawrence.

Curry vans ran the gauntlet
to Lidget Green and left
the unclean veg.

Years from Rusholme's
Golden Mile, plates
without cutlery, choice massala.

Batata harrara summer,
coriander evenings,
late bay-leaves.

Taj Mahal a sizzle
rumours of ingredients
could not allay.

Oil has nothing
to do with print
in a culture of entertainment.

This Taj's piquant sauce
is a slurry of ink
and Hammerton Street.